K B

Prayers in Reverse

by

Kayla Danielle Beard

@2023

Table of Contents

Dedication   1

Acknowledments   2

Introduction   3

The Creator   7

Happy Sabbaths   8

Those Men, They Say   9

Chruch Vibes   10

Cracks in the Armor of God   11

When I Do Cry   12

Wasted Waters   13

For My Mother   14

A Prayer in Reverse 15

Where We Are 16

Masochist 17

Stay Saved 18

A Girl Knows Nothing 19

The Journey Within 20

What "He" Might Have Me Do 21

An Honest Question 22

The Warmth Within 23

The Voice of my Creator 24

Blasphemy 25

Born Again and Again 26

Faith 27

A Moment of Gratitude 28

Hymn to the Divine 29

Reflections 30

I dedicate this book to my nieces: Nadia, Nazareth, Natalia and Eliana. Each of you has a beacon of truth glistening within you. Your spirit knows what truth feels like, how it smells and tastes and sounds. Listen to yourself and trust that which brings you closer to love, not fear or shame or guilt. If you can do that, you will always find yourself on the right path.

I dedicate this book to my ancestors, including those I cannot name, who dedicated their life to a religion like the one I was fed as a child. I have so much gratitude for the beautiful lessons I gleaned from many teachings in the Seventh Day Adventist church. Few spiritual traditions are complete trash, even if there are people who perpetuate harmful perspectives on the same teaching.

Finally, I dedicate this book to all the believers like me. After I renounced my first religion, it was challenging for me to accept the idea that any version of God was real. I prayed and I listened and I rejected nearly every message, questioning every spark of clarity that would come my way. I didn't want to just cling to the belief in God as a remnant of the spiritual beliefs I was taught, so I chose to search for truth without assuming that God would be a part of it.

Along the way, I found God again. (Like an old friend meeting me on the other side of a rickety bridge). I completely deconstructed my faith and reimagined what God is, how God moves, and how I commune with God.

Truth, in religion, is subjective. We desperately want a clear, objective reality but the nature of faith makes that dream an implausibility. A "truth" in one culture may be considered completely bogus to another. While we have tools and methods of validating some facts on this earth, the nature of God is a mystery scientists, spiritual leaders and philosophers all have yet to solve (not with consensus, anyway).

Yet, we keep seeking. To all those who have questioned their faith, or even abandoned it, but kept an open mind to the ever unfolding mysteries of life; to those who sought a deep spiritual connection free from the judgment and persecution which so often plagues religion: this book is for you.

Acknowledgments

Before all else, I must acknowledge my ancestors—those whose names I know, and those whose names I don't. Without you, I would not be here. To you, I am eternally grateful.

I also have to give thanks to my mother. Thank you for encouraging me to create. Without you, I would not have a story to share.

Thank you Austin, for being a consistent friend, a passionate creator, and an inspiration to me. Thanks for taking the time to really care for this book and for our friendship.

To those who read this book before it was published, thank you. You've done a service to me and to the readers.

Introduction

I grew up singing songs of salvation and surrendering my soul to Jesus Christ once a week on Saturday. At least, that's how my story began.

Jesus seemed less like a far-away God dwelling in a distant realm, and more like a close friend. This friend lived in my heart and wisely whispered in my ear thoughts like, "Don't take what isn't yours," and "Better to let go than hold a grudge." These words rooted in the soil of my soul, blooming in my mind on a regular basis. I lived my life as if the Son of God remained perched on my shoulder from day to day.

One summer afternoon, just before I began my freshman year of college, my mother told my two brothers and me that she was having doubts about her faith. She said she considered herself an agnostic now. I already knew the difference between agnosticism and atheism. Atheists believe there is no God, while agnostics choose neither to accept nor reject the concept of God. If you were to ask her again today, my mother might say she is more of an atheist.

For generations, beginning with her great-grandfather, my mother's family has been baptized members in the Seventh-day Adventist (SDA) church, a Protestant, literalist Christian religion. My father was also raised in the SDA church and my upbringing was heavily-influenced by my parents' spiritual beliefs.

There are many teachings that separate Protestant Christians from Catholics, and Protestant groups from one another. To briefly summarize a few of the many teachings in the SDA church, Saturdays are considered a holy day of rest (the Sabbath), the Protestant Bible is viewed as a literal description of historical and prophetic events, and believers who have died will not go to heaven until Christ returns.

Faith was always an important part of my life, but I also had doubts from the first time I read a copy of the Bible for myself. Even after interrogating numerous pastors about their faith in the ancient text, I was never fully convinced that every word in any translation of a book so heavily edited could be considered the infallible "word of God." Still, I always accepted the belief in God as a loving, omnipresent creator with little challenge.

After my mother decided officially to leave the church—a long and difficult process for her—my own subconscious doubts crept back to the surface. Poetry was my compass when navigating my way through the resulting storm of emotions.

In spite of all the emotional confusion I have waded through within the last decade of my life, I give thanks for every lesson I learned as a consequence of my mother's honesty in sharing her experience. It took courage for her to break away from a worldview she held onto for more than forty years. I imagine it took even more courage to be honest with her children about her change of heart, to say, "I was wrong," and "I've abandoned the beliefs that I once taught you as truth." The poem, "For My Mother," highlights the gratitude I have for the woman who taught me how to pray:

> *"You knew more than I ever could*
> *I still believe*
> *Your words carry sunlight"*

Still, there was within me a pinch of pain that accompanied the news of my mother's new religious views. Throughout my childhood, a piece of me had clung to the certainty that my family knew "the Truth." The idea that my certainty had become a fragile foundation my own mother could easily dissolve left me aimless in my quest for truth. As expressed in "Wasted Waters":

> *"In search of solid ground,*
> *I wade in the water.*
> *Faith floats away."*

Over time, I simply stopped believing the story I'd trusted since I was a toddler. It was difficult. At first, I did my best to search for the missing pieces that could bring me back to that familiar place of certainty and faith. I had been taught to tie my self-worth, my purpose for living, and my source of power to a figure whom I had believed was a living, physical being. Suddenly, I began questioning the existence of that being and, consequently, the relevance of my own existence.

When I still attended church regularly, there were moments I felt ashamed to even sit in a Christian sanctuary with so much doubt in my spirit. But I continued going anyway—my mind warped around a version of truth that never felt right in my heart—out of fear that I would no longer identify with the people who composed the community I claimed as my own. "Masochist" is all about those desultory feelings of guilt and shame:

> *"Shame is like an umbrella.*
> *They tell me*
> *Your mercy rains.*
> *Still,*
> *I feel inadequate"*

There were times along the journey when I questioned my desire to live. Until that period in time, I had always believed that I was born to serve the Christian God. Jesus was literally the justification for my existence. I didn't know what self-worth outside of my religion looked like, and I didn't know how to start searching for it.

Every role model I had ever admired placed Jesus at the top of his or her priority list. "Always put God first," they said, often using "god" and "Jesus" interchangeably. Without that sense of direction, I felt lost and alone. As expressed succinctly in "Where We Are," I questioned the nature of reality itself. My speculations were bleak:

> *"Is reality*
> *Hell"*

Still, I prayed and I searched for a new way of thinking. I studied texts I had never read, I learned from perspectives I had never thought to investigate, and I kept my heart open to the idea that God—the true creator—could be found if he or she existed.

Gradually, I chose to let go of the narrative I was born into and realized that another narrative made more sense. I came across the concept that Jesus was a character in a story, rather than a historical figure. This was a completely new way of thinking, but in my heart it felt truer than anything else I had been taught about God. Ultimately, I decided I could no longer call myself a "Christian" without feeling hypocritical. With that shift, I created space for my spirit to stretch and grow.

Despite my disillusionment with Christianity as a spiritual path, I have never stopped believing in my God. I have always believed in a complex, intelligent creator and I have always believed that my connection to a "higher power," whatever it seeks to be called, is incredibly valuable.

As "Born Again and Again" depicts, I now have a different understanding, a more embodied experience of God. It's difficult to explain:

"I can't explain
This heavy shell—it's something that
I think God lives within."

In the absence of doubt, there is self-acceptance. My spiritual practices and beliefs are more intricate and personal since I decided to open my heart and pray that the truth would find me. My spiritual journey has led me to discover more about the Earth and the many different cultures hereupon. Even more importantly, I have learned so much more about myself. If my soul winds up in Hell as comeuppance for all this enlightenment, then I'll be damned.

I am still unraveling the strange psychological consequences of my experience. The most unexpected and painful fact about my shifted worldview has been the grief. Jesus, a personal friend of mine, was lost to me and has become more like a casual acquaintance along my new spiritual path. I have been surprised and saddened by the necessary process of grieving the loss of Jesus from my life. The poems contained in this little book helped me to make sense of that grief and illuminate opportunities for self-discovery. I hope they can do the same for others.

I chose to call this collection Prayers in Reverse because every poem is meant to be read forward (top to bottom) and backward (bottom to top). This structure provided me with a stable container for my emotions, a tool to ground the gossamer messages I needed to pin down, as well as a parallel for the idea that faith and religion may be understood from multiple varying perspectives. My hope is that these words will inspire you, reader, to deeply consider the value of your own faith, no matter what you believe. I also hope that you will shine an inquisitive light on every unexplored corner of your worldview. May these words remind you that seeing the world from a different angle can be a beautiful and satisfying practice.

The Creator

God is
Only as far off as you decide
God is
Every voice that tells you not to hide
God is
Moving, breathing, living deep inside
God is
Floating in the wind beneath all wings
God is
Flowing in the rivers and the springs
God is
Present in each voice that dares to sing

I am
Embers of creation, pieces of light
I am
A cosmic fractal, a grape on a vine
I am
One with all things, a child of The Divine
I am that, I am

Happy Sabbaths

Way back when
I prayed often.
I smiled more.
I moved different, felt different.

On Saturdays,
When faith fell like raindrops

We used to pray together.
When you believed,
Hope wafted through the air.

I remember the

Dinners after church.
Gospel music
Choirs singing

Every weekend:
Before we fell,

Those Men, They Say

You never can trust those men
Laughing with their eyes, and cold inside.
They walk with shoulders swiveling
Up and back, reaching for the stars.
Their arms
Flag posts of promises and niceties
Those men,
We never can trust them:
Yet, even when they smile,
Teeth gleaming,
The sparkle of wealth,
Leached from the pockets of true faith,
Those men
Can never truly be trusted.
Rooted in the sweetest lie alive, they
Preach devastation to sell Christ's salvation.
With each word,
Those men,
Break the chains of earthbound faith.
Now, the old ways forgotten.
Fires pop up everywhere
The wildflowers, once, did bloom
Here
Faith used to be a sacred thing.

Church Vibes

Feels like magic
In this place:
Music feels like joy.
Melodies float
From faithful tongues
Here
I can feel Him
Smile
All I can do is
Listen
As my foundation crumbles?
Are they watching
Doubt choke my grin?
I feel
Cursed.

Cracks in the Armor of God

"Dear God,"
My mother is in the bathroom crying
    "Why?"
Is it only me who knows
The cracks in her bones
    Mirror
All the lies etched into her mind

I look to her
Trying to fix myself
        I bury my faith
At the bottom of a cardboard box
    My peace of mind
    I finally found

But somehow
    I lost
        Everything I loved

Along the way

When I Do Cry

No matter what.

           I hate crying in public,

Washed in waves of pity

From friends who think I need

           Comfort

I try to feel

           Grateful

Believe me, I am

           But

           It fills me with shame,

All the same.

I *hate* crying in public

           But

           I've always hated

           Crying in private,

Wasted Waters

In each tear,

A prayer swims.

This sadness is sanctuary.

Sinking scriptures

In search of solid ground,

I wade in the water.

Faith floats away.

Carried by Life's current,

As always,

Things change.

But

I once believed, too.

Because of you,

For My Mother

Mom,
You were always my
Strength.
You gave me
A roadmap for life.

I followed your example like
You knew more than I ever could.
I still believe
Your words carry sunlight.
Your thoughts water seeds.

In my mind,
You will always be important.
Though,
I know,
You are not always right.

A Prayer in Reverse

Amen,
Because all I see is space . . .

Are you there, God?
I'm tired of answering myself.
I've been praying ever since
I heard God was earless:
When I was a child
They told me.
My mind was tied in knots, so
I learned to tighten nooses
On reality.
I never could tighten my grip
On believing.
Maybe I just gave up
I tried to pray, but
When I looked in the mirror,
My face became fable.
My faith looked like fiction.
I started to think
Fear kept me faithful.
Dear God,

Where We Are

Is reality
Hell
Like an idea
Which haunts you
An apparition
Hell is not
Fire
Ocean of
Lava or an
Empty threat
Not an
Obligation
Hell is
Just as I'd expected

Masochist

Without fail,
My knees ache.
I kneel anyway,
Though prayer needs not knees.
My words fall
From careful lips.

    I quake
    For fear of my own thoughts.
    Shame is like an umbrella.
    They tell me
    Your mercy rains.
    Still,
    I feel inadequate.

    Within myself

I see
The scars
Left behind
Each time you
Tried to save me.
    You put nails in my hands.
I felt it when
I closed my eyes to pray,
Whispering, "in Jesus name."
It felt like
    A crucifixion
    I thought that I deserved

Stay Saved

What matters most

Is this

Everything

I used to believe

I find myself doubting

Now

I'm trying to grip faith

By its fragile throat

My trust hangs

From the edge of a cloud

My hope swings

Back and forth

To memories

I want to return

I want to be saved

But

I can't find my savior

A Girl Knows Nothing

About the gods I knew

Nothing.

Even when I dug real deep,
All I could find was
Too many questions.
I had
Only one way.
I knew
I couldn't stray too far
Into distant waters.
Traveling
Somewhere within myself.
I knew,
You were
Just like the sun
Blinding me
So everything was bright.
You gave me faith
Before I knew
What knowledge was.
My soul did tell me
After while

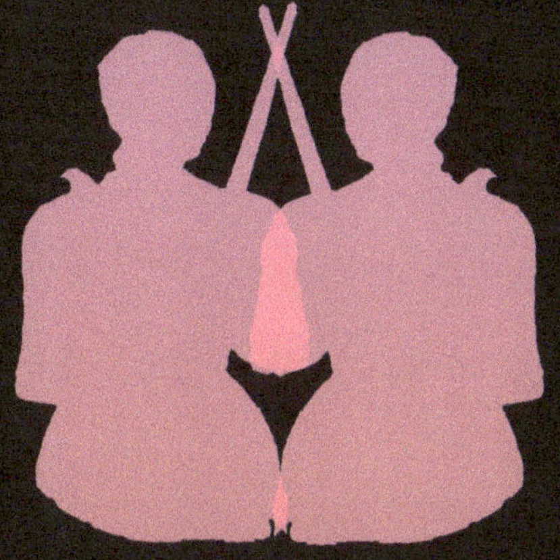

The Journey Within

A little bag of souls

      Buried in my blood

Has made me look for ghosts

The answer to my prayers

And in my quest for truth

      I think I met my demons

Skipping through my hell

  Torching my salvation

     In this righteous rage

  None could ever find

A better source of light

What "He" Might Have Me Do

Make me.
If ever you could
Live and breathe
You would have me sing
Praises, feed your spirit.
Like nectar on honeybees lips,
My faith glistens
An incandescent tower,
I send prayers up
By incense smoke.
The scent of my desires masked
And you promised to wash me clean,
But your blood was red as mine.
Baptism is the only salvation
You made me believe.

An Honest Question

What is a prayer?

But a desperate question?

When we cannot find the answers,

What do we cling to?

When life feels like a Cold Mother,

The world a barren bottle,

When every face looks stranger,

What is it we aim to be?

What is this endless breathing and

Why do we give thanks for it?

Each new day

We ask ourselves to appreciate

What little life we are given.

Only the gods might explain.

The Warmth Within

It's better inside
They tell me.
The winter is much colder than
The core of my own heart.
Cracked, just like
Drifting ice, no chance to melt,
I feel the Lonesome.

The hummingbirds within me
Are
No more.
I used to hum along.
I remember hearing songs
When I first shut my eyes to sleep
I thought I heard your voice, too.

Even in the silence
The noise kept me alive, and
Though my whole being rang
Melodies in ode to you,
I thought I was finished writing
For the love of God.

The Voice of My Creator

Carelessly

I once swung

From very old branches

On my mother's faith

My soul did sway

And does, to this day

Haunted my mind

To know that truth

"None of this is real."

My great-grandmother warned me

Before she let go

She gave us all we know

The oldest living root

On my tree of Salvation

Blasphemy

How could I
Repent?

Deep within me
It was always you

When I do
Remember how
I couldn't
Be without you

I wanted to(o)
Desperately
To change
How I thought you wanted me

The moment I heard
I knew
Humming in the background
You would always be here
My God

Born Again and Again

I think to myself,
I don't come here often.
These buildings look like ghosts,
Silhouettes of my foremothers.
I never thought I'd have to face
This feeling.

I can't explain
This heavy shell—it's something that
I think God lives within.
Though my faith feels like air
I know
We all must hold onto something.

In order to stay afloat
I can't throw my God into the river.
And so
I've baptized myself.
Again,

Faith

How can one define it?
Faith
How could I have lost my
Peace
I only wanted to find
Truth

Sadly, I did not know
Love
Deeper than the deepest
Sea
Under a translucent
Sky
I would gaze into the

Void
Revel in the endless
Bliss
Of embodying true
Joy
Now, I feel I know the
Fates
Of Each Soul—I've met the
Source.

A Moment of Gratitude

For every moment

I give thanks

That faith was all I had.

Lord knows

Though it wasn't perfect

My faith taught me love.

My mother taught me faith

Is the ultimate lesson.

Love for myself

Was like cash in the sludge

And every lesson since

Makes my spirit sigh.

The realization that

Every breath is God—

Carols in my soul.

Now, I can remember

Hymn to The Divine

With the greatest

I align

With the highest

I align

With purest love

I align

With the Divine

I align

Reflections

When I look back
On the path which brought me here
There never were any demons.
Instead, I found my peace
On the nightstand, coiled tight
In a dark room, by myself
I contemplated my own extermination.
Even then,
There was only light
On the inside.
There was only joy
At every turn.
I knew my truth would meet me
In the end,

Thank you for reading!

For speaking engagements, readings,
commissioned work or to learn more,
connect with Kayla at:
www.kdbeard.com

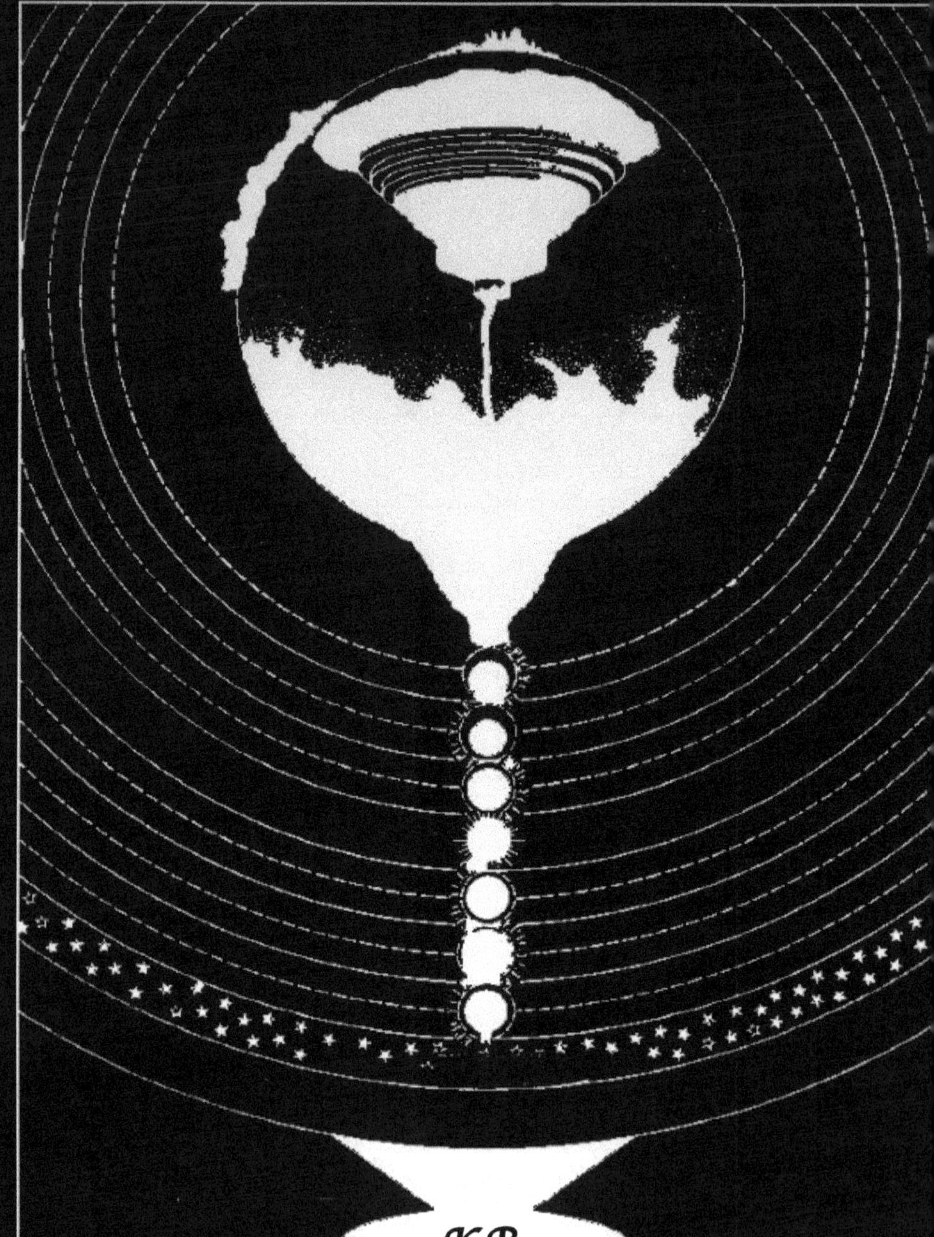

KB
Prayers in Reverse

9 7 9 8 2 1 8 1 6 0 8 8 3